Harpers Bus Memories in Colour
By Paul Roberts

Copyright IRWELL PRESS Ltd.,
ISBN 978-1-906919-56-6
First published in 2012 by Irwell Press Ltd., 59A, High
Street, Clophill, Bedfordshire, MK45 4BE
Printed by Konway Press

Most people living in the Cannock Chase, Aldridge and Brownhills areas before 1975 will have heard of Harper Bros (Heath Hayes) Ltd. This company, almost always simply referred to as 'Harpers' was synonymous with public transport in the area, taking many residents on their journeys to school, work, days out, tours and even on a summer Saturday coastal express service for a holiday. The company also put the name of Heath Hayes, a small Staffordshire mining village, on the national map as bus enthusiasts throughout the country took an interest in this well-known operator. Their mixed fleet amounted to over 50 vehicles, making them the largest independent operator in Staffordshire. They had buses bodied by their own workshops, ancient second-hand workhorses and purpose-built brand new vehicles.

I was living in Doncaster when I initially read about the company and paid my first visit to Heath Hayes on an enthusiasts tour. I already had my green conductor's Public Service Vehicle badge and decided that I would love to work for Harpers and sample the delights of their hugely varied fleet. (I will refer to the company as just 'Harpers' throughout the book; this after all was the style used, without the apostrophe, in some of their own adverts). On 14 April 1970 I drove my trusty Morris 1000 from Dudley (where I was at College) to Heath Hayes, asked for a part time job and, to my amazement after the briefest of interviews, was told to report the next day

to conduct the Bishopswood service! With Dave Box driving and under the watchful eye of a conductor called Fred, whose surname I cannot recollect, I started the job which would alter my life forever. In July of the same year I gained my PSV driver's licence and settled down to regular part-time work to increase my meagre teaching salary. Regular attendance was rewarded with a variety of work, mainly stage carriage but with occasional coach journeys as a bonus. I discovered that driving around the country was my preferred career and after three years went full-time, spending the rest of my working life in the bus industry. The first section of the book deals with the different vehicle types in use during my period working for the company. Next is a look at the different routes, contracts and private hires. The final part covers the farewell trip and subsequent takeover of Harpers by Midland Red in 1974, a company I continued to work for until 1986. After 40 years certain memories become blurred so I am grateful to my friends Stan Brookhouse and Steve Page, who also worked for Harpers, for filling in some gaps. Thanks also to Paul Anderson, Tony Hall, Stuart Turner and Bryan Yates for assistance in various ways and my wife Dot for her continued patience. All photographs are by the author.

Paul Roberts Leicester 2012

This was the view I yearned for as a working bus conductor – standing on the rear platform of a London Transport designed RT/RTL – a classic bus. Harpers had eight when I started working for them in 1970, and their carefully thought-out design, bell chords rather than pushes, and musical sound effects made working on them a pleasure. The conductors of these vehicles would have to remove/replace the upstairs light bulbs to prevent them from being stolen when parked overnight on the outside 'patch'. Notice the colourful advert on the side window for Skegness; another one at the front shows that the company requires drivers – some things never change!

This is the trip which fired up my enthusiasm for Harpers. I was still living in Doncaster during college vacations when, on Sunday 13 April 1969, the Doncaster Omnibus & Light Railway Society organised a tour visiting several Staffordshire Independents. Just visible, to the left, is our transport for the day, a Plaxton bodied Bedford minibus belonging to Premier Coaches of Stainforth. The double decker is a 1963 Guy Arab V which operated as a demonstrator for several years before being bought by Harpers. Its 72 seat Strachans body was unique, with peaked domes, heavily raked front and a rectangular rear end. It was fitted with a 4-speed semi-automatic gearbox and a Gardner 6LX engine. A top speed of 38mph made it slower than Harpers Leylands, but the low ratio rear axle gave it legendary pulling power maintaining the same speed 'uphill and down dale' according to many drivers, something eventually confirmed by myself. Because it arrived at Harpers in faded white 'demonstrator' livery she was always referred to as 'The Old Grey Mare'.

In the 1960s, many operators ran second-hand London Transport RTs and RTLs, which flooded the market as LT disposed of vast numbers of them. They had bought almost 7,000 of this type for use in and around the capital and many of them soon became surplus to requirements. These buses were the saviour of many an operator as their well designed and reliable features promised many years of further service despite their knockdown price. When I arrived at Harpers they still had four operational ex-London RTLs with Leyland chassis. Like many an enthusiast I was fascinated by these buses, images of which appeared everywhere in the 1950s. They were *the* London Bus until displaced by the now-famous Routemaster. This RTL, No.1 (JXN 349), intrigued me as it was a product of 1948 and I first saw the light of day in 1949! It was the only bus I worked on regularly that was older than me. It is partially framed by the front of one of its sisters while parked on the patch of land at the back of the Heath Hayes garage. The other RTLs in the fleet were, No.3 (OLD 820), No.4 (KXW 284) and No.7 (KYY 770).

Waiting at the Birmingham Carrs Lane terminus in 1972 is No.8 (BDJ 802) dating from 1951. It is about to load up on the 17.07 to Cannock, some 22 miles away. It was one of four RTs remaining in service when I started work for the firm. These AEC Regent IIIs came from St Helens Corporation who had bought 40 of them between 1950 and 1952. Ten years later they sold them off and Harpers obtained seven of them. Unusually they were built to full London Transport specification, making them identical to their southern counterparts, the only giveaway being their BDJ registrations and external livery. Their slightly lower than normal height of 14ft 3½in enabled them to pass under a low bridge in St Helens, fractionally too low for the standard height bus, 14ft 6in.

PRIVATE

SBF 233

Having made do with second-hand buses for many years the company bought a new Northern Counties 64-seat Leyland PD2/28 in 1962. No.25 (SBF 233) was delivered with a BMMO style 'tin-front' but, following an accident, it had a 'St Helens' front attached to the rounded Midland Red bonnet. This modification took place just before I started driving No.25 in 1970. The PD2/28 (one of about 40 PD2 variants) was a rare type having air brakes, synchromesh gearbox and the previously mentioned Midland Red front which was more common as an 8ft wide fitting rather than this 7ft 6in version. My friend Maurice Dickens wanted to do some part-time driving for the company. I asked Albert Harper if Maurice could take his PSV test with the firm and he said if I donated my time as an instructor he would provide the bus and the diesel. Procedures were less rigorous in those days! While practising test manoeuvres we took the bus to assorted locations around Walsall and Cannock Chase not normally associated with Harpers buses. This view features one of these sessions, which as well as providing good photo-opportunities did actually result in Maurice gaining his PSV licence.

In June 1965 Harpers finally obtained a licence to run through to the centre of Birmingham. Until this date they had to terminate their Cannock service at Kingstanding, on the city boundary, with onward passengers having to transfer to Birmingham City Transport buses. Increased demand for the through service resulted in the purchase of a pair of new Leyland PD2A/27s with Metro-Cammell bodywork. In this scene Nos. 27 and 28 (HBF 679/HBF 680D), delivered in January 1966, are flanking two much older single-deckers. The PD2s are showing signs of a hard six-year life and No.28 looks in need of a bit of attention. The two saloons both originated from Burlingham Coachworks at Blackpool with the classic curvy 'Seagull' body. By the time of this view they were both used on service-work and so the 1952 Royal Tiger No.50 (XRE 725) lost its shapely front end in 1967 to receive a bus-type front entrance. This in-house conversion replaced a centre entrance, typical for coaches in the early 1950s but impractical for bus work. No.59 (1293 RE) is one of two 1959 Guy Arab LUFs which retained coach seats throughout their lives, continuing in preservation to the current day.

Following the PD2s there was a natural progression to higher capacity 72-seat Northern Counties bodied Leyland PD3s in 1968 as demand for the through route to and from Cannock and Birmingham increased. A pair of manual gearbox PD3A/1s (Nos.24 and 26) appeared in March 1968, followed by a semi-automatic PD3A/5 (No.23) in May of the same year. This was notable in being the last PD3 delivered to an independent operator and all the more interesting for having a traditional rear entrance. This is my only view taken at the original Union Street terminus in Birmingham, which would soon be pedestrianised. These buses did not have spy-holes for the driver to see the destination blind as he wound it round, relying on a third party to assist. The news-vendor out of sight just ahead of the bus terminus gained a good working knowledge of the timetable and by the time the conductor got to the front of the bus the blind would be perfectly set, courtesy of the Evening Mail! No.24 (LRF 992F) waits for the 15.37 departure on a Saturday in August 1971.

The rear-engined era came to Harpers in 1970 with the arrival of two Northern Counties bodied Daimler Fleetline CRG6/6LXs, Nos.29/30, followed in the summer of 1971 by Nos.31/32 which were similar buses. The earlier pair seated 77 passengers whereas No.31 (BRE 311J) waiting for trade during a Sunday evening at Carrs Lane in Birmingham, had a luggage rack over the front nearside wheel arch which replaced two seats. My friend Steve Page, conductor for the shift, gazes up the street while three friends who had come to meet me lean nonchalantly against the boarded up shop front. My presence in the middle of the road has alerted one of the striding pedestrians. He is looking over his shoulder wondering what is so special about this particular bus! It is in 'as delivered' condition still sporting cream bands just below the windows. An ex-Birmingham City Transport Daimler Fleetline, now belonging to WMPTE, swings out of High Street and into Carrs Lane where it will emerge onto Moor Street Queensway opposite Moor Street railway station.

The final Daimler Fleetlines delivered to Harpers broke away completely from the previous specifications. They were CRL6s with ECW bodywork seating 74 passengers. CRL denoted that they were fitted with Leyland 0680 engines rather than the more common Gardner option. These two, Nos.33/34 (TRE 948/9L) soon became favourites with drivers. Their faster revving engines gave them a better turn of speed than their Gardner powered predecessors. Also their much lighter throttle springs made them far easier on the right ankle. Soon after the pair arrived in February 1973 I was allocated a Sunday shift on No.33. As I arrived in Cannock bus station, sister bus No.34 was in the offside parking bay. I took the opportunity to pose my bus alongside and obtain this view. Another feature unique to the pair was the fitting of Autofare ticket issuing equipment for one-man operation (there were no women drivers with Harpers at this time). The red 'Exact-Fare' boxes are visible through the nearside windscreens.

Although based at nearby Heath Hayes, the hub of most stage-carriage operations for the company was Cannock. We now commence a tour of all the regular routes starting with the trunk service, Cannock to Birmingham. Each arrival from England's second city had a 30 minute layover in Cannock bus station while its crew took a break. There was rarely a time during the day when at least one of Harpers newer buses was not available for a photograph in the parking bay. On this occasion one of the three PD3s, No.24 (LRF 992F) is enjoying a half hour break before returning to Birmingham. The first time I conducted one of these buses I was both surprised and pleased to discover that they were fitted with London Transport type bell chords in the lower saloon. This meant that the bus could be rung off from anywhere downstairs, although the driver did receive a few spurious bell-signals from passengers who thought it was some form of loose hand-grab!

Soon after leaving the bus station buses on routes 1 or 11, via Leacroft, would travel along Girton Road under the Cannock to Rugeley railway line. The bridge was plated as 14ft 3in, three inches *below* the standard height of a double-decker! On an enthusiasts trip in April 1973 Nos.11 (888 DUK) and 9 (BDJ 807) halt briefly to show the extremely tight clearance under the bridge; the old gasworks is just visible in the background. PD2 No.25 was fractionally higher than other double deckers and was likely to catch its roof on the bridge, so it was banned from using Girton Road. At this time the railway was freight-only but Cannock station was reopened to passengers in 1989 when through trains began running from Hednesford to Birmingham New Street. This scene can no longer be recreated. Girton Road, which at one time carried a bus every hour en route to Birmingham, has been bypassed and blocked off. Access under the bridge is now available only to pedestrians.

Another wholly changed scene still only a couple of miles from Cannock bus station. At this point Gorsemoor Road used to meet Cannock Road on the edge of Heath Hayes. The open fields have given way to the Hawks Green 'mini-town', a massive housing development, and the dangerous junction replaced by a roundabout a short distance away. No.32 (BRE 312J) is making the awkward turn onto the main road where visibility back down the A5190 was restricted because of the acute angle between the roads. It was custom and practice for the conductor to assist the driver in this manoeuvre by looking back towards Heath Hayes and giving the driver the 'all-clear'. On this occasion the bus is being driven by Joe Scott, who has just had to avoid my Hillman Imp parked near the junction, and conducted by Alistair Wilson. The doors have also been left open for extra visibility but if the bus was a half-cab the conductor would stand behind the driver and tap twice with a coin on the cab window when the road was clear. Not exactly text-book stuff but very helpful!

Routes 2 and 12 took an alternative route to Heath Hayes, and on towards Birmingham, 'via Cross Keys'. The pub in question is just out of sight to the right as Leyland PD2/28 No.25 heads up Hill Street towards Lea Hall Colliery, near Rugeley on the north side of Cannock Chase. The driver appears to have left the depot in a hurry as the bus still shows HEATH HAYES on the destination blind. This is obviously wrong as the said village is one mile behind the bus. On the left is Littleworth Road and in the background are the chimneys of the erstwhile Hednesford Brickworks. This site has recently been safeguarded as a nature reserve. The workmen, attending to a manhole in the middle of this crossroads, seem oblivious to any danger as traffic passes within inches of them on the wrong side of the road!

Former London Transport RTL No.3 (OLD 820) has achieved a good turn of speed as it reaches the bottom of the long descent down Hill Street from Heath Hayes. This time the Cross Keys pub is just behind the photographer but still out of sight. The 1954-built 56-seater is also heading towards Lea Hall Colliery to take the miners home from the morning or 'day' shift. The driver has taken the trouble to blank-off the destination but has not shown the correct setting of COLLIERY SERVICE which was available on all Harpers vehicles. Whilst these reliable workhorses were primarily used on contract work they would also often be found on local services, particularly as peak hour 'duplicates'.

My favourite PD3 was No.23, the only 2-pedal Leyland Titan in the fleet and very fast! The bus looks smart having recently been repainted from its original livery, with two cream bands, into a simplified single band style. It is heading through the centre of Heath Hayes, the nerve centre of Harpers operation, and passing The Talbot pub, notable even then as one of the last in the area serving Worthington E as a cask ale. There are plenty of pedestrians about in an era when people shopped locally and car owners bought vehicles made in the UK. Harpers bus garage was at the top end of the street, on the right, near the distant tree. The company did not have a monopoly of services through the village. WMPTE route 47 from Lichfield ran though to Cannock at almost exactly the same time as the Harpers service 12. Many of our crews attempted to beat the 'blue bus' to try and pick up the passengers waiting on this section.

The next settlement along the route was Norton Canes. Post-war housing development is visible beyond the pylons. The village was at one time notable for the large number of collieries within its boundaries. Jerome K Jerome, author of 'Three Men in a Boat' was a famous son of Norton. One of the local pits was the Jerome Colliery owned by the same family. On this day I was in charge of No.4 (KXW 284), another ex-London Transport RTL, this one dating from 1950. I was running light and realised that the sun was perfect for a photograph, which explains the lack of a driver in the cab. Unfortunately the view also confirms that I had failed to set my destination blind correctly! Beyond the pool is an embankment which holds back the Chasewater Reservoir, a feeder for the Wyrley & Essington Canal. On the top of the bank was the fledgling Chasewater Railway which is still running today. From 1970 I would occasionally see locomotives steaming along this section at weekends.

1968 Leyland PD3A/1 No.26 is just over the border from Staffordshire, and in the then new West Midlands Metropolitan County at Brownhills West. In this 1972 view the gap on the blind is where the words 'Union Street' have been painted over following the alteration of the Birmingham terminus to Carrs Lane. Conductors always filled in their waybills at the previous Pear Tree Inn stop as WMPTE controlled the fares for the rest of the journey. The building behind the bus is the Wilkin Inn, although many older passengers would ask for 'The Monkey'. Legend has it that a past landlord kept a monkey in a cage at the end of the bar, giving rise to this nickname. This scene is only half a mile beyond the previous view but the land between has changed completely with the building of Britain's first toll motorway. The new elevated Hednesford Road motorway bridge over the M6 Toll now gives a good view of the previously hidden Chasewater Railway site. The railway sidings and station were relocated as they used to stand on the route of the new motorway.

RTL No.4 is approaching Brownhills having driven down The Parade. It has just come from the A5 Watling Street near the southern end of Chasewater. Seven miles and twenty five minutes after leaving Cannock, the bus is entering a lay-by which was a main timing point. If buses arrived at this stop early crews were supposed to wait for time before setting off down Brownhills High Street, a major source of passengers. The Hussey Arms is visible through the trees to the rear of the bus and on the opposite side of the Chester Road was a small Jet petrol station.

Some 15 minutes further along the route, after passing the Shire Oak pub and a timing point at Streets Corner, buses reached the town of Aldridge. About a quarter of all services terminated here, circling the roundabout and returning to Heath Hayes or Cannock. PD3A/1 No.24 (LRF 992F) has just dropped off its passengers in Northgate and performed this manoeuvre. Don Green, the conductor, is hanging off the platform and has yet to assist the driver in altering his destination display. The Northgate stop was also where a peak-time local route, the Leighswood Estate Circular, terminated. Most crews disliked this service because of its short length and repetitive nature – three round trips in a morning and 14 in the afternoon, timed to complete each circuit in just 12 minutes. Because of this it was known as the 'Whizzer' and an unofficial Blue Riband time evolved with less than 8 minutes once claimed on a quiet trip! The large pub in the background is the Elms Hotel, a major feature in this relatively small town centre.

The junction of Portland Road and Anchor Road was the next stop along the route after the Elms Hotel. This area has much changed since this view was taken in 1974. Daimler Fleetline No.32 (BRE 312J) is crewed by John Woodhouse and Steve Page. The bus has just travelled along Portland Road, now part of a relief road leading to the modern Anchor Road Bypass. At this time Harpers still had a small filling station and coach garage just behind the photographer on Anchor Road. 45-seater Bedford VAM/Duple No.65 (OBF 593J) was the sole allocation at Harpers' Aldridge garage where Sid Jones was the resident driver. The BMC car is parked on a major road junction unmarked by yellow lines and bears a Staffordshire registration; this county was one of a handful to use the original A-suffix registrations.

Leyland Titan PD3 No.24 descending Aldridge Road in Streetly near the Hundred Acre Road bus stop. The vehicle is in less than pristine condition and it is surprising to find No.24 out on service with its front offside wing in such a crumpled state. Unusually it also carries an external advertisement. This view was taken just after the Midland Red takeover in 1974 and possibly interest in vehicle presentation was waning. At the top of the hill is the square office block of the Streetly Works, where Bakelite plastic items were manufactured. This long-gone factory was a huge source of work for Harpers with buses or coaches serving all three shifts and others being required to transport staff working normal office hours; indeed my first-ever driving shift with Harpers was to and from the works for the 22.00 shift change.

For many years the terminus of the Harpers service was at Kingstanding where passengers had to get off and transfer to City Transport buses for the last six miles into Birmingham centre. Following the extension of the route in 1965 this inconvenient and time-consuming change was no longer necessary. Licence restrictions meant a further bonus for through passengers, for the service was limited-stop and only allowed to set-down once it was within the city boundary. This speeded up the journey even more as there were only seven stops in five miles. As the through service gained in popularity peak-hour reliefs were added to the schedule and in this view No.25 is a duplicate bus descending Kingstanding Road just before the Circle. There are parked cars just out of sight to the left, which explains the stream of vehicles all hogging the offside lane. The silhouette of a Daimler Fleetline can just be made out on the crest of the hill as the 'service' bus follows.

We have finally arrived at Birmingham Carrs Lane, terminus for all departures from the city after 9 January 1972. Fleetline No.29 had recently had its first repaint in this 1973 view having been delivered in two cream band livery. Along with ex-St Helens No.8, Fleetline No.29 is waiting to make the 17.07 service 11 departure to Cannock which always had a duplicate on weekdays. It picked up further relief buses at Aston Six Ways, Kingstanding Circle and Aldridge, resulting in a convoy of five assorted vehicles all vying for pole position as their crews headed towards Heath Hayes and the end of their shifts. The reader will note that the building next to the RT is in various states of dereliction and demolition in other views within the book.

Carrs Lane was also the terminus for the Birmingham to Boney Hay route 944, jointly operated firstly with Walsall Corporation and then with the West Midlands PTE. This route was normally operated by double deckers but occasionally a 51-seat coach would be used by Harpers. Sometimes there would be a conductor and on other occasions the driver used a hand-held Setright machine, and a cash bag, as an impromptu one-man operation. No.61 (SBF 447J) was one of three 1970 Plaxton Elite/Leyland Leopard PSU3/3Rs with 4-speed manual gearboxes and 2-speed rear axles. The numbering system always replaced previous fleet numbers so the three in the batch were 61, 64 and 78. As a result of this policy the highest number allocated seems to have been No.80!

During a farewell tour of the routes on Sunday 21 April 1974, Leyland Titans Nos.25 and 23 make a brief photographic stop at Kingstanding Circle. Soon after Harpers first penetrated Birmingham in 1965, the 944 route was introduced. Monday to Friday had departures from Birmingham at 10.50, 14.50 and 17.50 (all operated by Harpers) and 17.05 and 17.15 (Walsall Corporation). Saturdays saw five more evenly spread departures entirely operated by Harpers. After leaving Kingstanding the next scheduled stop was at Stonnall Turn, some six miles along the A452 Chester Road. Licence restrictions meant that from this point onwards the service was set-down only, making it popular with conductors (who could cash up and just ring bell signals for the next 40 minutes) and drivers who were guaranteed a fast drive. No.25 frequently appeared on service 944 but was delivered before the route started operating so always ran with a blank destination and a board in the cab window.

No.28 is displaying **LIMITED STOP** and enjoying a high speed run along the Chester Road towards Birmingham on service 944. The high route number reflects Walsall Corporation's policy of using the 900 series for all its 'Limited Stop' services. The bus is sharing the road with a fascinating selection of British built vehicles on this bright day in summer 1973. The bridge carries the freight-only line from Walsall to Sutton Park. Hugging the white line ensured safe passage for double-deckers under this bridge as demonstrated by the shirt-sleeved driver.

Gentleshaw Hill, on the southern edge of Cannock Chase, is visible beyond No.28 as it makes its final circuit of the Boney Hay terminal loop. Burntwood, Boney Hay and Chase Terrace are in Staffordshire and were traditionally served by buses to the adjacent towns of Lichfield, Cannock and Walsall. The population of the area doubled at the end of the 1960s as it became an overspill for Birmingham. This led to the introduction of the 944 service, making a direct link to the city. Originally there were just two early morning departures suitable for commuters and a mid-morning one for shoppers. These were balanced with three appropriate return workings. Demand led to an extra two trips per day but over the decades this has dwindled to just one commuter journey per day, at the time of writing, renumbered X56.

Lichfield was the north-east extremity of Harpers stage carriage operations. This service never advertised its official route No.3 during my time with the company. It ran approximately every two hours and a large portion of the route was through rural country lanes. It took in the historic village of Wall, then Shenstone and Stonnall before heading for the larger town of Aldridge. Some journeys were extended to Kingstanding for connections into Birmingham. On 26 April 1970 I conducted the last ever Sunday service on this route, surprisingly still crew operated. A few weeks later the bus-fronted Burlingham Seagull/Leyland Royal Tigers continued to be regular performers on this route, and I have left No.50 (XRE 725) briefly unattended to take a photograph. In common with many firms, Harpers had started to introduce driver-only operation to its quieter services and a Setright Speed hand-cranked machine can be seen through the windscreen. Crew changes on this route necessitated the use of either the company's Morris 1000 van or, if unavailable, a full size bus or coach to transfer the staff the seven miles to and from Heath Hayes garage.

Although the core service from Kingstanding to Lichfield was provided by single deck buses, a double decker duplicate would operate via a slightly different route from Wall on schooldays. This brought students into Lichfield and was due to arrive at 08.50. The scene is re-created on the Farewell Harpers tour when RTL No.4 (KXW 284) and RT No.8 (BDJ 802) take a break in the bus station on 21 April 1974. This view also shows the HB roundel, on the back of the bus, sometimes used in lieu of the full name. Along with all staff I was issued with a similar lapel badge. Midland Red operated several routes in and around the city and from 1954 to May 1971 had a garage on Trent Valley Road housing nineteen vehicles. Following its closure, BMMO buses still served Lichfield from garages as far away as Bearwood, Stafford, Sutton Coldfield, Swadlincote and Tamworth. In 2012 half the bus station bays have been given over to car parking, a reflection of modern transport trends.

In 1972 Harpers received their last new single deck bus. This was a Willowbrook bodied Bedford SB5, seating 40 passengers. This surprise purchase resulted from several factors. The 50% bus grant had recently been introduced, and the company got a good discount as this 'off the shelf' bus was added on to a large order for Bedford coaches. Managing Director Albert Harper told me that the overall cost was less than £1,500 – a bargain too good to refuse, even allowing for prices of the day. Soon after delivery one driver (believed to be Steve Clarke) observed that it looked 'just like a bread van!' That nickname stuck with No.47 (NRF 420L) throughout its life with Harpers and into Midland Red days. I took advantage of a quiet trip one afternoon in the summer of 1974 to pose the 'bread van' on Lynn Lane, Stonnall, en-route to Shenstone and Lichfield.

Shenstone was on a spur from the main route so buses would enter and leave the village via Station Road whether travelling to or from Lichfield. On arrival at The Railway pub the bus would circle the war memorial and stop at the main village stop on this service. The Saturdays only West Midlands PTE service to Walsall ran every 90 minutes and made seven trips. At 14.05 it clashed with the two-hourly Harpers service so in 1973 I took this opportunity to record the two buses together on this once weekly occurrence, yet again to the surprise of my passengers! No.47 was equipped with an exact-fare box, similar to the one visible through the windscreen of the double decker. No.50L (EDH 950C) is one of Walsall's short Daimler Fleetlines with Northern Counties 70-seat bodywork, but by now transferred to WMPTE ownership. They had smaller Gardner engines than normally used in Fleetlines and were designated CRG6LW.

Another rural service ran for many years from Cannock to Brewood. Subsequently it was extended to Kiddemore Green and Bishops Wood, a journey of twelve miles, for which 50 minutes were allowed. By 1974, the year of this photograph, the service had been cut back to Calf Heath, served on just three days a week. There were also about a dozen short workings to Cannock's Longford Estate on Mondays to Saturdays. These trips were scheduled for just six minutes each way and were often made by buses operating services which otherwise would have had waiting time in Cannock bus station. Such a working accounts for Northern Counties bodied Daimler Fleetline CRG6LX No.32 (BRE 312J) providing 75 seats for such a lightly used service. This view was taken at the main Ascot Drive stop on a very quiet evening trip. On return to the bus station, No.32 would continue on the much busier Birmingham service.

Another example of this operation features No.33 (TRE 948L), one of two ECW bodied Daimler Fleetline CRL6s delivered in February 1973. This is also on the Longford Estate route but this time at the Gorsey Lane terminus. With the advent of one-man operations the service was altered to a circuit at the outer terminus, thus avoiding a reversing manoeuvre. These two Fleetlines were used on certain Sunday services, the only day that the Birmingham route was regularly one-man operated. They were fitted with exact-fare vaults and modern Autofare ticket machines which could issue any ticket priced from 1p to 99p, more than enough to cope with fare values of the day. These buses were always favourites with drivers. With their responsive Leyland 0680 engines and light throttle pedals they had a much better turn of speed than their heavy, plodding Gardner equivalents.

Five trips per day were extended to Calf Heath, where the buses operated a large circle round the local lanes, before going back to Cannock. A further three buses continued along the whole route to Bishopswood, returning down the same roads. On Saturdays a through service ran hourly, providing for seven departures. A stroke of luck one Saturday early in 1971 led to my obtaining this view of both buses on the route passing on Vicarage Road, Calf Heath. This was just before the crossing of the then new M6, just south of Junction 12 at Gailey. The battle-scarred 1951 Leyland Royal Tiger No.49 (VRF 630) carries a 44-seat body built by Harpers in 1960 and based on Metal Sections frames. The oncoming vehicle is No.58 (1292RE) a Guy Arab LUF with Willowbrook 41-seat coach bodywork, complete with a manually operated hinged door.

Later the same day, No.58 has arrived in Brewood, driven by Pete Lowe, and is dropping off passengers from Cannock. Even in the early 1970s these narrow streets were struggling to cope with the ever-increasing traffic whilst passengers had to contend with minimal footpath space when boarding and alighting at this point. There were never any bus stop signs here on Stafford Street – the locals just knew where to get on! The destination display shows KIDDEMORE GREEN, the previous terminus. The route was extended to Bishopswood in 1965 and was withdrawn a mere six years later. It was common practice for Harpers to use these Guy coaches on rural routes, drivers of the day becoming adept at handling their 5-speed overdrive crash gearboxes.

The last addition to the service routes started on Monday 24 May 1971. This was the Motorway Express from Hednesford and Cannock to Birmingham, utilising the recently opened M6 Motorway Midlands Links section. The route had a premium flat-fare of 4/- (20p). This was thirty per cent more than the stage carriage stopping service but travelled from Cannock to Birmingham in 50 minutes rather than the 77 minutes on the 'old' road. Regular performers on the route were the four 1968 Duple Commander/Leyland Leopard PSU3/3Rs. These were Nos.68, 69, 75 and 76, all fitted with appropriate destination blinds. Additional stopping points were listed on a windscreen board, as shown by No.75 (ORF 459F) waiting to depart from Hednesford bus station. West Cannock No.5 Colliery was still open nearby, so 16 ton mineral wagons can be seen in the sidings behind the bus station. The commuter timings soon became popular and the 51 seats were often full leading to standing passengers being carried on the M6! The service was licensed as limited stop stage carriage so this unusual practice was legal at that time; fortunately it never led to any problems.

Off peak journeys were sometimes operated by the Burlingham Seagull Guy/Arab LUFs (sometimes even Bedford VAMs or SB5s) so it was fitting to use a Guy and a Commander/Leopard for the farewell tour in April 1974. They are at the stop listed as Saredon, Holly Bush on Wolverhampton Road near Cheslyn Hay, the last main stop before joining the M6 at Junction 11. After take-over by Midland Red the route gained the service number X98. Later this became the X30/1 after it was extended across Cannock Chase to Rugeley via the main road or Slitting Mill. Daily congestion on the motorway seriously affected punctuality and for a while it was re-routed through Walsall via the A34. After the re-opening of the Hednesford to Birmingham railway line in 1989 most regular passengers deserted the coach service and it was withdrawn.

Contract services for a variety of factories, collieries and schools provided Harpers with a steady income all year round. One route to GEC at Witton, Birmingham, used an RTL every weekday. This was manned by a part time Harpers crew who then worked full time at GEC before bringing their workmates home along the route to Heath Hayes. Every weekday afternoon the patch behind Heath Hayes garage would steadily empty as the fleet departed to contract pick-up points throughout the area. No.71 (ARE 712J) a 1971 Bedford SB5 with Duple 41-seat bodywork is heading off to Streetly Works, not far short of the Birmingham City boundary, to bring workers home at 16.30. This view is in mid-1974 when all operations continued unchanged but vehicles carried ON HIRE TO MIDLAND RED stickers in their windscreens, before full licence transfer took place.

Lea Hall Colliery was about one mile south-east of Rugeley along the Armitage Road. In 1972 the adjacent Rugeley B power station was opened, taking coal direct from Lea Hall by conveyor belt. Miners shift changes required vehicles from several local operators, including on this occasion RTL No.3 and PD2 No.27 from the Harpers fleet. The bus and coach park was directly opposite the canteen block so an early arrival ensured a 'cuppa' before taking the miners home. Another staff bonus in the canteen was the sale of very cheap soap and towels, a 'perk' extended to the bus crews on site. One of Harpers buses would arrive at the colliery with just the driver on board. A passenger would ring the bell signals until the bus reached Heath Hayes. Here it would pick up its official conductor who signed on over an hour later than the driver. The crew would then continue to the destination at Shelfield Spring Cottage, near Rushall.

Buses running along Armitage Road would normally travel non-stop to the colliery. On this occasion enthusiasts have hired No.3 (OLD 820) to do a tour of local independents and I was lucky enough to be the driver. The reason for stopping is that just to the right of the RTL are the premises of Middleton's of Rugeley, who were then operating buses and coaches. At the time of this view, in the early 1970s, the railway bridge in the background carried the link from Rugeley Trent Valley to Walsall and Birmingham, which saw regular freight trains. The only passenger trains at this time would be Sunday diversions from Stafford to Birmingham, avoiding the Stour Valley line and regularly hauled by English Electric class 40s. In years to come fortunes would change and since 1997 Rugeley Town has had through trains to Birmingham after extension of the Hednesford service, itself reopened in 1989 and branded The Chase Line.

Another carefully-posed photograph, during a private-hire trip, shows the tight clearance (just two and a half inches – theoretically) between the roof of RT No.9 and Handsacre railway bridge. This section of track between Stafford and Lichfield is part of the West Coast Main Line. It had not long been electrified at the time of the photograph in 1972. This view would be substantially unchanged for the next 30 years but between 2004 and 2008 the quadrupling of the Trent Valley section of the line caused much disruption and change to Handsacre and Armitage. No.9 was considerably rebuilt by Harpers, fitted with platform doors, fluorescent lights and fixed upstairs front windows. A wind-down communication window was fitted between the driver and the lower saloon. These modifications made this bus the normal choice for double deck private hire work at the time.

Another daily destination for three contract vehicles was the 'Ever Ready' Four Ashes works, right alongside the Stafford-Wolverhampton railway line, about one mile south of Gailey, near Penkridge. Every weekday afternoon two coaches and a double decker would perform a three-point turn at the end of the drive and then line up ready to take the workers back to various parts of Cannock and The Chase. This is the calm before the storm in mid-1974 as 150 workers are about to appear and board the buses. All three vehicles are in Harpers livery, with 41-seat Duple bodied Bedford SB5 No.73 (WRE 336G) followed by a slightly bigger 45-seat Duple bodied Bedford VAM70 No.62 (FBF 794H). Bringing up the rear is one of the relatively new ECW bodied Daimler Fleetlines. After dropping off the last passengers the double decker would travel out to Boney Hay, and make the 16.51 journey to Birmingham on route 944 and the 17.50 return. The absence of the other two drivers means that they are either chatting on the rear bus or, more likely, cadging a cup of tea from the canteen staff before taking them home!

Another Bedford VAM70, No.63 (FBF 791H) drops off its passengers at Cannock bus station before heading off towards Heath Hayes garage and the end of the shift. Yet again the four 'FBFs' had consecutive registration numbers, 791-794 but were numbered 63, 77, 74 and 62 respectively, filling in freed-up numbers. One contract ran to Ever Ready in Park Lane, Wolverhampton, opposite the Guy works. An employee/steward took a 'fare' from each passenger and paid it in to their company. Wolverhampton Corporation ran the Cannock to Wolverhampton route 21 and was preparing an objection to this contract. The basis for this was that fares were being collected contrary to the license restrictions leading to abstraction of revenue from the 21. On 3 December 1973 Midland Red took over the 21, renumbered it 872 and duly took over the court case. In 1974 MROC then took over Harpers and found that they were objecting to themselves operating their own contract. The case was rapidly dropped!

Having photographed No.63 in the bus station I then dashed round the corner into Cannock town centre to obtain this view of the coach, with the door still open, disappearing down Stafford Road, on its 'depot run'. This road was actually the A34 which ran through the middle of the town and Market Place as it continued south. In the 21st Century this view is unrepeatable, the area having been pedestrianised. Through traffic now uses the Ringway to pass round the back of the town centre.

The rush back to Heath Hayes was to avoid being too far back in the refuelling queue on Hednesford Road. Drivers also were required to park their vehicles before they could finish the shift. Each bus or coach would move up to the garage, turn right across the road, temporarily blocking through traffic, then reverse on to the diesel pump. Even with lower traffic levels in the early 1970s this manoeuvre was not appreciated by the locals. Another odd feature was the need to entirely circle the small roundabout by the Five Ways pub, visible in the background. The acute left turn from Cannock was too sharp for a bus (no powered steering then) so they swung right round the island to join the queue. On this occasion another Bedford VAM, No.77 (FBF 792H), has arrived from a journey on the 944 Boney Hay service; the shift running board is visible behind the windscreen wiper. These 45-seat high-step coaches were not appropriate for stage carriage but the view demonstrates the flexibility shown in vehicle rostering. It is interesting to see how prices have increased over the intervening years with brand new flats in Heath View advertised from £6,450.

Under normal circumstances, the newest coaches had regular allocated senior drivers and were confined to private hire work. On this occasion in the autumn of 1972 I was driving a Leyland PD3 from Birmingham to Cannock when I met Joe Slatcher taking 'his' coach to Streetly Works. I always carried my camera so while loading at Anchor Bridge, Brownhills, I took this photograph from the cab (which explains the high view point). A new coach on a contract was a fairly uncommon event and probably occurred on this day because Joe had a private hire job straight afterwards. No.55 (MRF 420L) was a short PSU4B/4R Leyland Leopard seating just 45 in its 33ft long Duple Viceroy body. Similar coaches were No.51 (LRF 220K) normally driven by George Brown and No.56 (MRF 421L) which was allocated to Joe Scott. The Warreners Arms in the background closed in 1999 and became a MacDonald's, which in turn shut down in 2003 and is still boarded up at the time of writing.

The other three Leyland Leopards delivered in 1972 were 51-seat PSU3B/4R versions built to the more usual 36 ft length. All six coaches in the batch were 2-pedal control with 5-speed semi-automatic air-operated gearboxes – a complete change for Harpers coach fleet. With the expansion of the motorway system Harpers realised there was a need for both heavy and lightweight coaches, according to the job in hand. These three heavyweights were No.52 (MRF 417L) allocated to Jack Poyser, No.53 (MRF 418L) with Maurice Meek and No.54 (MRF 419L). There is uncertainty as to the regular driver of this last vehicle. Some of the fleet also carried TUDOR ROSE COACHES on the destination roll, a Sutton Coldfield company whose vehicles and licences were taken over in 1960. Nos.54-56 were actually registered to this company. Although the scene looks pleasantly rural it is actually the back of Harpers 'patch' looking over the remains of Coppice Colliery which closed in 1964 some eight years before this photograph.

Coach tours organised by Albert's sister, Mary Harper, accounted for a lot of business. I started full-time with the company in summer 1973, and by June 1974 was entrusted with a full load of holiday makers for a week-long tour to Teignmouth in Devon. As usual I recorded a selection of views including this one of seated passengers waiting for me to take them on an afternoon excursion. We all stayed at the Bay Hotel on Powderham Terrace with this view across The Den, as the gardens are known. At that time several large hotels still traded on Den Crescent, to the left. In recent times nearly all of them have become luxury apartments. This was the period just after Midland Red took control of Harpers so No.77 carries a small ON HIRE TO MIDLAND RED sticker in the windscreen. This gave me the advantage of being able to use fuel and washing facilities at the Greenslades garage in the town and Devon General at nearby Newton Abbot. All three of these firms were by then part of the National Bus Company.

Private hire work accounted for a large percentage of coaching, particularly in the summer. About two-thirds of the 50-strong fleet was made up of coaches. On this occasion I was taking a school party on a one-day field trip to Snowdonia, the ultimate destination being the Llanberis Pass. We had a break at a very cold and slightly damp Swallow Falls near Betws-y-Coed. An early start is reflected by the presence of just two cars to keep No.56 (MRF 421L) company. This is because most sensible tourists would just be considering leaving the comfort of their lodgings as it is still only breakfast time!

The last new vehicle in the Harpers fleet was No.67 (PBF 199M), a Leyland Leopard PSU5/4R with Plaxton Panorama bodywork. As the only 40ft long, 55-seat coach it promptly earned the nickname 'Big Bertha'. She was bought from dealers stock and therefore had a modified livery with much more cream than usual. On this occasion No.67 is operating an advertised Sunday evening mystery excursion from Cannock bus station and has already picked up at many places around the local area. The Bedford SB5 behind is acting as a relief. The numbers of passengers involved show a bygone era when cars were less common and people were not frightened to go out at night. In the summer the company also operated Saturday express routes to a large number of destinations including Blackpool, Torquay, Weymouth, Clacton, Great Yarmouth, as well as many more places in North Wales through to Pwllheli and Llandudno. These services often required two drivers – a great opportunity for new, recruits, such as me, to learn the ropes from more experienced men. Holiday fortnight brought such a flood of passengers that many extra vehicles had to be hired in, particularly from Salopia of Whitchurch in Shropshire.

During my early years with Harpers any major recovery work was left in the hands of an old Morris Commercial lorry. In 1973 the company took the surprising step of cutting down RT No.10 (BDJ 808) into a towing wagon and wrecker. Earnest discussion appears to be taking place between driver Roy Meek, engineer Len Edwards (right), and several other unidentified staff while Tony Cater looks on from the left. Originally, after conversion, it carried Staffordshire trade plate 361 RF but in this view after the Harpers takeover it is carrying borrowed Midland Red Central Works plate 413 HA. No.11 is parked against the back wall where damage to the front peak is clearly visible. A driver took it into a section of garage only high enough for single deck vehicles and the damage sustained was enough to ensure subsequent withdrawal and scrapping of this unique bus.

The next few pages show Harpers buses getting 'out and about', away from their normal territory. The combination of Harpers interesting fleet and the close location of other Staffordshire Independents led to several enthusiast tours being operated during my five years with the company. My status as driver and fellow-enthusiast meant that I drove several of these trips, including this one in April 1973. So many people booked that we had to run a relief, allowing both passengers and drivers to travel on No.11 and No.9 along different sections of the route. Whieldon's Green Bus Service had its headquarters at Rugeley but a quarter of the fleet of about 30 vehicles were based here at Uttoxeter. The Harpers buses are flanked by two Willowbrook bodied vehicles. On the left is an ex-Stratford Blue PD2/12 with 63 seats, No.30 (TNX 455) acquired in 1967, and on the right No.16 (44 AUW) an AEC Reliance 2MU3RA 41-seater bought from London operator Birch Brothers in 1970. Both were withdrawn before Green Bus sold out to Midland Red on 5 November 1973.

Double deckers were allowed to have occasional adventures in pre-tachograph years. At the end of the summer term in 1974 two such buses have been allowed to 'escape' to Twycross Zoo. Just four miles from No Man's Heath, where Staffordshire, Leicestershire, Derbyshire and Warwickshire all meet, the Zoo is convenient for excursions from several local counties as reflected in the vehicles present. On the right, from the East Midlands, is Trent No.540 (DRC 540J) a Daimler Fleetline CRG6LX with Alexander 77-seat body which is next to Harpers No.29, the bus I had brought from Heath Hayes. Nottinghamshire-based Barton Transport's No.1319 (WRR 357M) is a 53-seat Duple Dominant/Bedford YRT and just visible is a Midland Red BMMO S23, yet another ordinary service bus this time with 51 seats. For most schools the number of seats available was more important than the luxury they provided, seat-belts in PSVs being a future dream at that time.

This tour was particularly exciting for me, combining my first Yorkshire and Midlands firms in one trip. I was a member of both the Midlands Omnibus Preservation Society and the Doncaster Omnibus & Light Railway Society which joined forces for this excursion. Two completely different Burlingham bodied Guys were to be used, although they both had Gardner engines and crash gearboxes. No.59 (1293 RE) was taken to Doncaster, where it met up with Blue Line WWX 671, a Guy Arab IV, and photographs were taken here in Waterdale. The two buses then commenced a tour of local independents with Mick Fowler and me driving, not necessarily the correct vehicle! Having got permission to take No.59 on its longest jaunt for some years the coach seemingly 'disappeared'! It transpired that Albert Harper had secretly arranged for the Guy to go to Harpers High Green Works in Cannock, where Madge, the coach painter, had applied an immaculate new topcoat to our steed. This represented the company and MOPS in the finest way imaginable and, surprisingly, only a few weeks before Harpers sold out to Midland Red.

Another special repaint emerged from High Green when fellow enthusiast and driver Steve Clarke asked Albert Harper if we could take an RTL on the then new Trans-Pennine Run from Manchester to Harrogate in August 1973. We were delighted (and amazed) when he said 'Yes' and this was the result. No.7 (KYY 770) although nineteen years old, had recently been fitted with a new engine so was the clear favourite to survive such a challenging 270 mile round trip. For the first time in many years No.7 was reunited with one of its London Transport family and a direct comparison could be made with a London RT. My sister and her friend are admiring the bus as it stands on The Stray at Harrogate, the shine between the decks showing the reflection of RT238. Somehow a genuine London Transport radiator badge adorned the radiator of No.7 for the occasion. The journey was completed without incident and yet again Harpers kindly provided the diesel.

Another side to the Harpers generosity showed itself when maroon half-cab coach HVJ 583 needed its MOT renewing (in those days privately-owned preserved buses could be licensed as a private car). I was part-owner of this 1951 Wye Valley Leyland PS2/3 which was equipped with a Harrington body complete with celebrated dorsal fin. Albert Harper let us park the coach, gratis, at the garage for several days and permitted Ray Wood, a Harpers mechanic, do the necessary work (in his own time) using the pit at the rear of the patch. I took the opportunity to record the period and happily the new MOT certificate was duly obtained. Eventually I gave up my brief dalliance with preservation and, along with other co-owners, sold this magnificent machine to MOPS member David Wheatley who has kept the coach in running order ever since.

I decided that teaching was less fun than PSV driving and moved into full-time Harpers employment in August 1973. Sadly during the following spring the announcement was made that Harpers would sell all their PSV operations to Midland Red and Harper Bros (Heath Hayes) Ltd would become solely a property-owning company. The changeover was set for Monday 22 April 1974. The Midlands Omnibus Preservation Society felt that the occasion should not pass un-noticed and we quickly arranged a tour of all stage carriage routes on Sunday 21 April. The plan was to use four appropriate buses on four tour phases. The bookings just kept rolling in! With just under 90 passengers wishing to commemorate the demise of this well-known operator, we finally needed reliefs on all sections and on the run to Bishopswood, *three* 41-seat single deckers. The whole line-up of nine vehicles spread wider than my camera viewfinder and at this point passengers are gathering for the first section of the event. At the request of Harpers no fares were charged for this mammoth tour, just donations made to the Heath Hayes church organ fund – a final kind gesture from the family and company.

The plan was to traverse the main Cannock to Birmingham route first, so the pair of Leyland Titans set off together and made photographic stops at key points en route. This early stop was on the A452 Chester Road where it forms Brownhills High Street. As was typical on a Sunday in 1974 the streets were absolutely deserted, because apart from newsagents and the occasional cafe everything would have been shut. The vehicles were carefully chosen as Leyland PD2/12 No.25 was the first new Leyland Titan in the fleet and No.23 was the last PD3 for Harpers – indeed the last for any British independent.

Having visited Birmingham city centre we then returned along the 944 Boney Hay route. Both buses were well known for a handy turn of speed and gave a good performance on this fast limited stop route. Another reason for the choice of No.23 was that it was the only semi-automatic Titan in the fleet and so the sound effects were very different from its manual transmission sisters. Notable by their absence the good citizens of Oak Lane, Boney Hay must have been unmoved by the rare sight of two buses together, even though the route 944 never ran on a Sunday. At least it meant that the enthusiasts could capture images of this historic last-trip without disturbance!

Two more phases used a pair of RT/RTLs to Aldridge and Lichfield (page 29) and finally two coaches on the Motorway Express (page 37). This final phase ran quite late because the schedule for the day proved more than a little ambitious and over-optimistic! This was due in part to the number of photographic stops made during the earlier trip to Bishopswood. For this we used the 'bread van', No.47, sandwiched (if that's the right word...) between the two flat-fronted Royal Tigers No.50 and No.22. Here the convoy has stopped in Brewood, the main village on the route. It will be noted that since the earlier view of this location, the Lion Hotel sign has been removed – hopefully not by a souvenir hunter on the tour! By this time, there were no Harpers services to Brewood at all, so Stafford Street was witnessing a rare, if harmless invasion. Only a few years previously, in the mid-1960s there would have been seven Sunday journeys on this route.

After the full takeover on 7 September 1974 a number of original Midland Red buses were transferred in to Heath Hayes garage, along with some of their managers and inspectors. This scene at Four Ashes now has just one Harpers coach, on paper No.2274, but yet to gain its new number-transfer. Behind is a Ford R192 with Plaxton Derwent 45-seat bodywork, one of a hundred of this lightweight type bought for rural routes. Although only three years old, their noisy front-mounted engines and erratic brakes meant that they were generally disliked by our drivers. Bringing up the rear is a BMMO S16 built at Midland Red's own Central Works. With 52 seats they were used as replacements for the 56-seat RT types. Although they had 4-speed crash gearboxes married to relatively small 8.0 litre engines (rather than the 10.5 litres of their successors) they felt good and solid and were generally liked at Heath Hayes – at least the driver and conductor could have a chat during quiet periods.

All change at Cannock. Two 1971 Daimler Fleetlines show their 'before and after' treatment. I was in charge of No.2232 and keen to get comparison shots of buses in the two liveries whenever the chance arose. The whole Harpers fleet was renumbered, by the addition of 2,200 to the original two digit number and routes were all given new numbers, mainly in the 800s. For a time old and new fleet and route numbers ran side by side as in this view. While a rapid repaint programme was instituted some of the old 56-seat RTs and RTLs actually returned to all day service covering for absent Leyland Titans and Daimler Fleetlines. The 830 service to Rugeley represented another change; Midland Red buses from either Stafford or Tamworth including this S17 No.5570 (AHA 170B) now served the route which until 5 November 1973 would have been operated by Green Bus of Rugeley.

Two years on and most of the fleet has been repainted. A snowy day finds Harpers oldest Leyland Titan, now No.2225, looking a little cold and forlorn and in need of a destination blind. By chance the double decker to the rear is No.439 (JOX 439P) one of the last two buses ordered by Harpers. These were delivered direct to Midland Red in March 1976 and fitted with modified destination blinds including three-track number apertures. Along with sister No.440 these two Fleetline CRG6LXs became Midland Red's final double deck class of two and designated D14. Traditionally during winter the coaches were used far less and a proportion of Harpers fleet would be de-licensed and stored at their Stafford Road garage. Following their takeover Midland Red used the winter months to repaint all 26 coaches in time for the 1976 summer season.

Staffordshire was one of a few licensing authorities which issued single letter registrations, so 1031 E stands out as being unusual. My good friend Tom Owen, sadly no longer with us, would tell of how, in the past, he had taken this coach through London's Hyde Park as a short cut. This was against the byelaws and one day he was stopped and warned not to do it. A few days later he repeated the misdemeanour and was stopped again by the same policeman who, ironically hadn't recognised Tom but had remembered the single 'E' registration. Once he saw that it was Tom again suitable recriminations followed! Even if a little 'down at heel' this view of a classic Burlingham Seagull rear-end, carrying full ornate Harpers lettering, is a fitting final memory of a much-loved and much-missed company.